Cool-Doo Math

03

[GRADE 1 AND 2]

www.cool-doo.com

Andrew Feng

First Printing: 2015

ISBN: 978-0-9938371-2-8

www.cool-doo.com

Jack

Cool-Doo

Sleepy-Doo

To know the adventure of Jack and his gang,
please read *TUM* - The Unmoved Mover.
www.t-u-m.net

Dr. Green

Dr. Z

Jr. Z

To know the adventure of Jack and his gang,
please read *TUM* - The Unmoved Mover.
www.t-u-m.net

Contents

What Will I Take Out?

A Eat one bag of TUM Chips.

B Clean Cool-Doo's room.

C Take out the trash.

D Wash dishes.

Jack, you have to take out a tag from this bag without looking. Each tag has a letter on it. Take a look at the chart above!

TUM Chips! TUM Chips!

Bad Idea, Jack!

ANSWER

SOLUTION

Cool-Doo has put tag B in the bag 20 times, more than any other tags he put there.

So, Jack will most likely take tag B, which says to clean Cool-Doo's room.

The correct answer is B.

TUM-GPS

Jack, Cool-Doo and Sleepy-Doo were delivering pizzas with TUMCOPTERS!

They earned

$2.00

for each pizza
they delivered.

Jack delivered 10 pizzas.

Cool-Doo delivered 5 pizzas.

Sleepy-Doo delivered 2 pizzas.

ANSWER

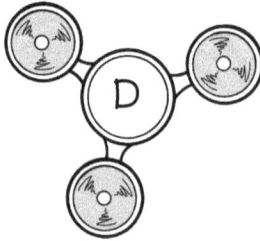

SOLUTION

Jack delivers 10 pizzas and each one costs $2.00, so $2.00 × 10 = $20.00.

Sleepy-Doo delivers 2 pizzas, so $2.00 × 2 = $4.00.

Cool-Doo delivers 5 pizzas, so $2.00 × 5 = $10.00.

Now, add these! $20.00 + $4.00 + $10.00 = $34.00.

The correct answer is D.

How Long is the "Canal"?

A
30 sailboats
B
17 sailboats
C
18 sailboats
D
25 sailboats
Boom! Splash! TUM Sailboat Fight! Bam! Whoosh!
TUM
TUM
TUM

ANSWER

SOLUTION

All you have to do for this question is add all of the distances.

5 sailboats + 12 sailboats + 13 sailboats = 30 sailboats.

The correct answer is A.

Fish, Turtles, and Frogs

ANSWER

SOLUTION

First, to figure out the number of legs all 6 turtles have, do 4 legs × 6 turtles = 24 legs because each turtle has 4 legs.

Now, this is the tricky part - the 11 fish don't have any legs! So, you don't have to do anything here.

Finally, each frog has 4 legs, so 4 legs × 4 frogs = 16 legs.

Now, add up the 2 numbers. 24 legs + 16 legs = 40 legs.

The correct answer is C.

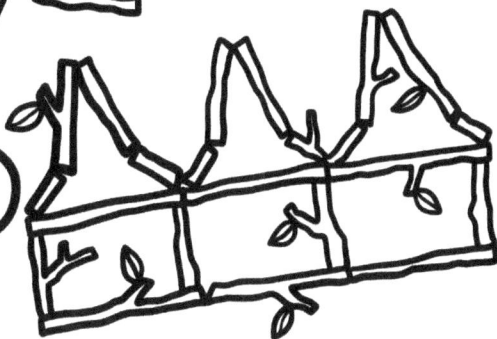

ANSWER

SOLUTION

Jack has already finished making 3 houses. He needs to make 7 more.

Each house is made of 8 sticks, but the connected houses share 1 stick. So, each additional house only needs 7 sticks.

$7 \times 7 = 49$.

The correct answer is D.

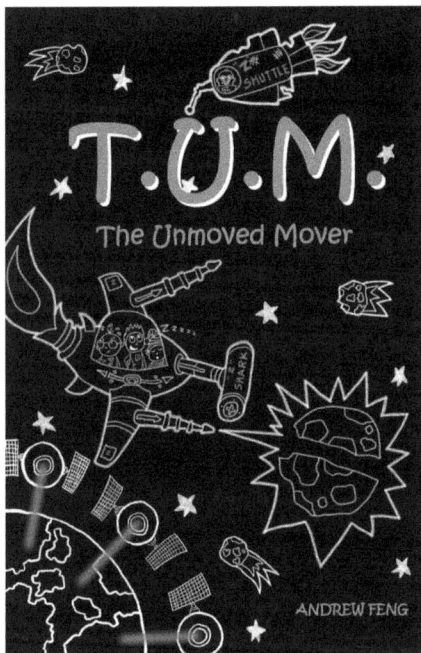

Do you get along with your brother?

Jack doesn't!

Although he has always expected to have a brother to play with, he finds his dream of brotherhood shattered after he gets a really "special" one. This special one always impresses Jack's parents. Plus, this special one also has a special friend of his own, and things always stir up crazily.

Finally, a chance comes for Jack to impress his parents. His hometown is placed in danger while he and the other two special guys are in a space camp, and he only has one night left to become the hero. But, of course, his "special" brother also wants to be the hero.

The clock is ticking...can they make it? And which one will make it?

(www.t-u-m.net)

" A *lively* adventure that *charms* and *delights!* "

- KIRKUS REVIEWS

About the Author

"Myths can be true; fairy tales can be true; even lies can be true. So, why not my dream?"

Who made up this quote?

Andrew Feng did!

He was born on a snowy day.

He loves to draw, to read, and enjoys playing Ping Pong and video games.

He wants to be an awesome-ordinary guy.

www.ingramcontent.com/pod-product-compliance
Lightning Source LLC
Chambersburg PA
CBHW060545030426
42337CB00021B/4441